GW00859469

It really ties the room together

T. Wobblecocksmas

&

M. Hissfatchick

FOR T.

Happy 49th Birthday

You really tie the room together

CONTENTS

INCLUSION

'We are all included'

'Unless you are intolerant of the tolerant, in which case the tolerant will become intolerant of you in their tolerance of others you are intolerant of, even if it's not what they are intolerant of but what they force on you in their tolerance'

CANCEL BREXIT

'That's it!'

'Cancel Brexit'

'Hand me the free visa and I'll wear the chains!'

'I refuse to be inconvenienced at the border and pay an extra fiver on my trip'

'Outrageous'

MICKEY ROURKE

'Mickey Rourke is fucking irritating'

'Sounds like a knockoff Sylverster Stallone displaying the wisdom of Eric Cantona during an epileptic fit of twatspeak'

DEMOCRACY

'I have voted for the party that might retain some remnants of democracy and will not build gulags'

'They will still fuck people up the arse'

'But they will use some lube at least'

'The others want to go in dry with a horse cock'

GOD

'God works in mysterious ways i.e. in a way that suggests he is either:

    a.   Imaginary
    b.   Is real, but is a level 1000 master of trolling'

IT REALLY TIES THE ROOM TOGETHER

GENDER

'Did you assume my gender?'

'I always do. I always assume you're a very handsome, fat lesbian'

'You had me at "very"'

CORONAL MASS EJECTION

'A coronal mass ejection is a non-gender specific emission that should not be objectified with a highly sexualized term that stigmatizes and leads to social violence towards celestial bodies. You are an enabler of such violence!'

MILKY SHOWERS

'You talk a lot of shit for a guy in cumshot distance'

THE VACCINE

'It is expected to be an initial 15 shot dose, followed by boosters every 1st, 3rd and 4th Tuesday of each month except April, when it will be every Wednesday.

Side effects may include "almost death", "close to death", "Wow, that was close, I almost died", "Oh shit, I'm dying" and "Death". Possibly also breasts'

AIRLINES

'23 kg = 50 £
26 kg = Are they taking the piss?!'

ANITA SARKEESIAN

'Did you hear Anita Sarkeesian is broke?''

'No… But like herpes… She'll be back'

TAKEN

'I have a very particular set of skills. Skills I have acquired over a very long career of being a cunt. Skills that make me a nightmare for people like you. If you come out for drinks tomorrow and Saturday, that'll be the end of it. I will not look for you, I will not pursue you. But if you don't, I will look for you, I will find you, and I will give you an impromptu and inappropriate reach around!

RESTAURANT

'I have booked a table for 7:30 on Saturday''

'What kind of restaurant?'

'One with tables'

'Chairs and the lot?'

'Oh yes! It's proper posh! Probably food and all!'

'Will you give me the location of this posh place or do people speak of it in hushed voices?'

'I shall send a coded message by pigeon precisely 34 minutes before'

'Will Enigma be enough to decode it?'

'The message shall be disguised as bird shit to avoid detection'

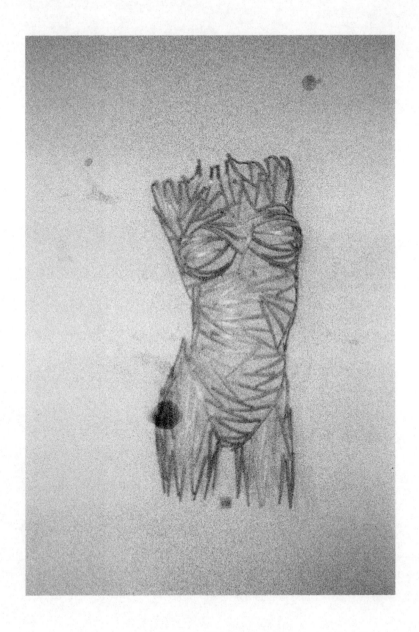

PRIVILEGE

'A man should feel privileged to die for a woman who doesn't give a fuck about him, to protect a society that blames him for all its ills, for a system that takes from him to give to those who have not earned from their own labour. And if he dares to complain then he deserves all the criticism he shall inevitably receive… and more. The lucky bastard!'

FAT SAUSAGES

'I was at a Tommy Emmanuel concert just now. Absolutely fantastic!'

'No way would I ever be able to do finger work like that, at least not on a guitar with my father sausages!'

'Obviously I meant fat sausage fingers. Father sausages sounds like something you get from going to Catholic school!'

COMING TO THE UK

'Will this be your first time to a civilized country?'

'It will be my first time to a pretentious country, that's for sure'

'There is nothing pretentious about our vast superiority above all other nations!'

'We have only the finest retards residing on our fair shores!'

fin

Printed in Great Britain
by Amazon

14914397R00031